# Following the Blood Trail from Genesis to Revelation

*Why Jesus had to die and what it means for us*

by Sylvia Bambola

Heritage Publishing House

For information contact:

**Heritage Publishing House**
heritagepubhouse@gmail.com

**Sylvia Bambola**
sylviabambola45@gmail.com

ISBN: 978-0-9657389-0-3
ISBN-10: 0-9657389-0-6

All Scriptures taken from Holy Bible, King
James version, Cambridge, 1769

*Also by Sylvia Bambola*

**Fiction:**
*Mercy at Midnight*
*The Babel Conspiracy*
*The Daughters of Jim Farrell*
*The Salt Covenants*
*Rebekah's Treasure*
*Return to Appleton*
*Waters of Marah*
*Tears in a Bottle*
*Refiner's Fire*

To

My children and grandchildren,
with love

# Table of Contents

Chapter 1 ........................................................ 7
Setting the Stage ........................................... 7

Chapter 2 ..................................................... 19
Following the Blood Trail in Old Testament
.................................................................... 19

Chapter 3 ..................................................... 43
Following the Blood Trail in New Testament
.................................................................... 43

Chapter 4 ..................................................... 55
But what does that mean for us now? ........ 55

# Chapter 1

# Setting the Stage

The Bible is like a treasure chest full of multi-layered gems and nuggets. But sometimes it can be more like buried treasure, you have to dig. Even so, the hunt is always worthwhile. First, you get the surface story. Then further digging often reveals types and shadows, clues pointing to other things. Often there are prophecies as well; some fulfilled, others yet to be.

But before digging in, it would help to understand that before time there was eternity. And something terrible happened in eternity past. A rebellion of unimaginable scope disrupted God's perfect order when Satan, a top-ranking angel, began making accusations against God. The Bible doesn't tell us what those accusations were. We can only imagine the evil things said about God's character, about His motives, perhaps even His fitness and right to rule. But whatever they were, they had to be convincing lies because one-third of all the angels joined Satan in his rebellion.

But while we don't know what Satan said, the Bible does tell us his motive. He wanted to be like God and to take His place!

## So, what was God to do?

He could have easily destroyed the rebels. After all, they were created beings; *His* created beings. But that would leave Satan's lingering accusations to possibly foment another rebellion among those angels still loyal.

It was a predicament.

How was God to once and for all illustrate His true loving character, and lay to rest all those lies and accusations perpetuated by Satan? And how was He to do this while, at the same time, allowing Satan to expose *his* true nature?

Since God knows the beginning from the end and everything in between, He knew what was necessary. He knew what it would take to fully restore His kingdom. And He knew it would come at great cost.

God's plan was brilliant, magnanimous, and terrifying all at once. He would create a dimension called time, containing a set span of seconds, minutes, hours, days, months, and years in which He would unfold His plan and display His true nature while exposing Satan's, and thus repair the torn fabric of His kingdom.

Genesis 1:1 opens with, "In the beginning, God . . .." In the beginning of what? God has no beginning, and neither does eternity. The Hebrew word here for *beginning* is *reshiyth* and means the first or best of a group, the beginning of a series.

And what did God do in this "beginning of a series"? He created the heaven and the earth. But the very next verse says, "and the earth was without form and void, and darkness was upon the face of the deep." Since God never creates anything void and without form, what is happening here? A simple word study using a *Strong's Concordance* and a *Theological Wordbook of the Old Testament* gives us the answer.

First, the Hebrew words "without form and void" are *tohuw* and *bohuw*, and mean a desolation, a waste, a worthless thing. But aside from *tohuw* and *bohuw* used here in Genesis 1:2, these words are only used together twice more in the Bible: Isaiah 34:11 and Jeremiah 4:23. In both cases, they explicitly refer to God's judgment.

Next, that word *darkness* in "and darkness was upon the face of the deep" gives us an even clearer picture. That word in Hebrew is *choshe* and literally means darkness, misery, destruction, wickedness. So, something happened between verse one and two of Genesis; something evil that caused the destruction and desolation of the earth, making it a worthless thing.

And finally, looking at the Hebrew word *was* in the sentence "and the earth was without form and void" is *hayah*. It's in the pluperfect tense indicating a past action. So, the more accurate translation would be, "the earth **became** without form and void". Or another way of saying it could be, "the earth was without form and void because it became that way".

Furthermore, God Himself tells us something important about creation in Isaiah 45:18. "For thus saith the Lord that created the heavens, God himself that formed the earth and made it; he that established it, he created it **not** in vain, he formed it to be inhabited; I am the Lord and there is none else."

That word *vain* is *tohuw*. It's the same word used in Genesis 1:2 meaning to lay waste, a desolation, a worthless thing.

So, what is God saying here? He's saying He's the creator. He made it all. There's no one else. And He didn't create it *tohuw*. He didn't create it a waste, a desolation or a worthless thing.

Now, going back to Jeremiah 4:23-27 where both *tohuw* and *bohuw* are used together.

Prior to these verses, God tells Jeremiah He is angry with Judah for their wickedness. At that time, the twelve tribes were split into two groups. The ten northern tribes were called Israel. The two southern tribes were called Judah. It is to these two southern tribes, to Judah, that God directs this prophesy, and foretells what He plans to do. But the prophesy is in the form of a vision of what happened in Genesis 1:2 to make the earth without form and void, indicating that He is going to do this same thing to Judah. So, God is using something that has already happened to illustrate what is going to happen.

And the vision is extraordinary in that it shows there was life on earth prior to the six days of creation. It says: "I beheld the earth, and lo, it was without form and void, and the heavens and they had no light. I beheld the mountains, and lo, they trembled, and all the hills moved lightly. I beheld and lo, there was no man (indicating this was before the creation of man) and all the birds of the heavens were fled. I beheld and lo, the fruitful place was a wilderness and all the cities thereof where broken down at the presence of the Lord and by his fierce anger. For thus hath the Lord said, the whole land shall be desolate, yet will I not make a full end."

Jeremiah's vision indicates this happened before man was created and that God, in His fierce anger, partially destroyed the earth making it "without form and void". But He did not destroy it completely, just like He wouldn't completely destroy Judah.

So, we see that the earth was inhabited prior to the six-days of creation and had cities. Were they the type of cities we envision today? There is no way of knowing because the Bible doesn't say. But that word *cities* in Hebrew is *ayar* and means a city, so they could be. But it also means a settlement or a place guarded by a watchman. And in these cities, settlements or places, there was even a Garden of Eden, as we shall see.

But how do we know Satan was on earth prior to the six says of creation? Because, in Ezekiel 28, God tells us he was. In this chapter, God chastises the **prince** of Tyrus for his wickedness. This was an actual person. It's also a prophetic type of the anti-Christ.

However, a few verses later (vs 12-19) God begins talking about Satan. He calls him the **king** of Tyrus, someone who is apparently controlling the prince of Tyrus which indicates that the future anti-Christ would also be controlled by Satan.

This is not the first time God directs His message to an actual ruler which then turns into a message about Satan. He did it when addressing the king of Babylon in Isaiah 14 and when addressing the mysterious Assyrian in Ezekiel 31.

We see it repeated here in Ezekiel 28:12-19 where God shifts from the prince of Tyrus to the king of Tyrus, or Satan. God talks about how perfect and beautiful Satan was. How he had been in Eden, the garden of God, and covered by precious stones. He called Satan the "anointed cherub that covereth". That word *covereth* is *sakak* and means a cover, a hedge, defend, defense, which is what a watchman does. He keeps watch over a certain place to protect it, to defend, to cover it as a hedge of protection. Remember, one definition of *cities* was a place guarded by a watchman.

Sylvia Bambola

Apparently, Satan had charge of the earth prior to his fall. He was the watchman. This may explain why he was still in the Garden of Eden after his fall and after the six-days of creation, and why he wanted to tempt Eve to sin in order to regain his authority.

Some Bible scholars believe that the first earth was destroyed sometime after Satan's rebellion due to God rendering a partial judgment which not only caused damage to the earth but caused Satan to lose his exalted status. But Satan's final judgment won't come until after Jesus' earthly 1000-year reign.

These same Bible scholars believe there is a literal gap between Genesis 1:1 and Genesis 1:2, and call it the Gap Theory. They believe that God, beginning in Genesis 1:3, was **restoring** the original earth rather than creating it.

To further back this up, Genesis 1:28 tells us that after God created man, He gave him the charge to not only be fruitful and multiply and have children, but to *replenish* the earth.

According to *Webster's New World Dictionary* plenish means to fill up, stock. While replenish means to fill again. Here, the Hebrew word for *replenish* is *mala* and is the exact word used when God, in Genesis 9:1, commands Noah to **replenish** the earth after the flood destroys everything. So, on two separate occasions God commands man to replenish the earth; the first time in the garden, the second time after the flood. He's basically telling them to restore the land, to cultivate the soil and plant. To make the earth flourish again.

Some scientific evidence, such as carbon dating, fossil records, and the age of certain rock formations, suggest this is an old earth. While other evidence, like the oldest reef, the Great Barrier Reef, being less than 5,000 years old, the earth's slowing rotation, and the declining magnetic field, all point to a young earth. Based on the Gap Theory, we can understand how both can be true. There is no contradiction.

We know Satan was already a fallen angel when we first see him in the Garden of Eden tempting Eve because he came to her as a serpent, making him a deceiver. And he lied to her, making him a liar.

Yet God created man knowing Satan would continue fomenting rebellion on earth, and knowing that man, too, would rebel. He also knew that when Adam and Eve disobeyed, they would lose the dominion over the earth which He had given them. He knew their sin would permit a legal deed transfer to take place in the spirit realm and put Satan back in control or at least partial control. That's why the Bible calls Satan the "god of this world".

## We are all living in a timeline,

a timeline set by God, Himself, and one that will last only until His full plan is accomplished; the plan to reconcile both heaven and earth back to his perfect order; the plan to uphold His holy name and character.

And it involves blood.

# Following the Blood Trail

# Chapter 2

# Following the Blood Trail in the Old Testament

Genesis 3:1-22 details the sin of Adam and Eve. After they disobeyed God and ate of the forbidden fruit, so they could be "gods," Genesis 3:7 tells us, "And the eyes of them both were opened, and they knew that they were naked, and they sewed fig leaves together and made themselves aprons."

That word *naked* in Hebrew means to make bare, to be cunning, to be crafty. In other words, Adam and Eve didn't just realize they weren't wearing clothes, they saw their craftiness. They had lost their innocence. And to cover up their nakedness, their craftiness, their exposed sin, they sewed fig leaves together and made aprons.

It's interesting to note that that word, *aprons,* in Hebrew means a belt, girdle, armor. But it also means to be afraid. So, Adam and Eve, afraid of what God would do when He saw their sin, their craftiness exposed, tried to cover it up. And from that time to this, man is still trying to cover up his sins by means of his own handiwork, his own solutions, his own good works. Every religion, except Christianity, tries to show men how to work their way back to God; how to sew aprons. While only Christianity shows how God worked His way back to man.

## God doesn't want aprons

His requirement is very different. After Adam and Eve sinned, Genesis 3:21 tells us that, "Unto Adam also and to his wife did the Lord God make coats of skins and clothed them."

In order to obtain these coats, God had to kill an innocent animal. In short, it was God Himself Who shed the first drop of innocent blood thus establishing from the very beginning in Genesis the criteria for covering sin: innocent blood.

Adam and Eve's sin did not take God by surprise. John the Baptist, in John 1:29, called Jesus "the Lamb of God which taketh away the sin of the world". And Revelation 13:8 talks about the "Lamb slain from the foundation of the world," showing God's foreknowledge not only of man's original sin but also of what His intended solution would be.

So, the killing of an innocent animal in the Garden of Eden is the foreshadowing of what is to come.

## The next time scripture talks about blood

is in Genesis 4:3-7 when Cain and Abel make a sacrifice to God. Abel's offering was the "firstlings of his flock", a blood sacrifice. Cain's was "the fruit of the ground" or produce. Genesis tells us that, "the Lord had respect unto Abel and to his offering. But unto Cain and to his offering he had not respect."

Why? Because Abel understood what pleased God. The Bible doesn't tell us how he knew. More than likely his parents told him what happened in the Garden of Eden and how God covered them with animal skins. At any rate, Abel understood that a pleasing sacrifice to God was one of blood.

In Genesis 4:7 God tells Cain if he does what's right, he'll be accepted. God wanted to accept Cain. That was His heart. But Cain didn't understand God's heart, nor did he try. Cain is a perfect illustration of man trying to please God according to his own understanding, his own ideas, his own efforts, by the work of his own hands instead of doing it God's way.

In addition, Cain offered cursed fruits. God, in Genesis 3:17 said, "cursed is the ground for thy sake." And fruits from a cursed ground are *cursed fruits.*

So, not only did Cain fail to take the time to understand what type of sacrifice pleased God, he actually offered cursed fruits. He, like his parents before him, tried to sew an apron. It's easy to see the parallel between what Cain did and the scripture in Isaiah 64:6 which says, "But we are all as an unclean thing, and all our righteousnesses are as filthy rags".

## God was setting up a pattern

with Cain and Abel, and showing us a fore-shadowing of a greater covenant. But Cain refused to learn the lesson, and out of anger and jealousy, kills his brother, Abel. Of course, God already knew what Cain did when He asked in Genesis 4:10, "What hast thou done? The voice of thy brother's blood crieth unto me from the ground."

That word, *voice*, in Hebrew means call aloud, a voice, a sound. Here, blood is equated with life, having its own voice and speaking. Not a sound or language we can hear, but one God can.

## The next blood episode: Genesis 7:2

Noah is preparing to fill the ark and God gives this command: "Of every clean beast thou shalt take to thee by sevens, the male and his female, and of beasts that are not clean by two, the male and his female." So, Noah was told to take seven pairs of clean animals but only one pair of unclean animals.

Notice that Noah already knew which animals God considered clean and those He considered unclean long before the Law of Moses was instituted. Again, God had been establishing the groundwork for the blood covenant.

Then, in Genesis 8:20-22, after the flood waters recede and Noah leaves the ark, he offers one of every clean animal (fowl and beast) as a sacrifice. And God is pleased and does the following: He removes the curse from the ground. That's why, later, various types of produce were acceptable sacrifices in the Jewish temple. Then He tells Noah he can now eat the flesh of animals (Genesis 9:3-4) but forbids Noah to eat or drink blood. He says, "But flesh with the life thereof, which is the blood thereof, shall ye not eat."

Later, in Leviticus 17:10-12 this restriction is again repeated, and the reason given: "For the life of the flesh is in the blood and **I have given it to you upon the altar to make an atonement for your souls: for it is the blood that maketh an atonement for the soul.**"

Here, God spells it out. Only blood can make an atonement. Only blood covers sin.

Under the Levitical Law, a whole system of animal sacrifices and blood handling was set up. Blood was holy and reserved only for God.

After Noah's sacrifice, God tells him, in Genesis 9:5-6, that if a beast or man takes the life of a man, the blood of that man or beast will be required. Then God gives the reason: "Whoso sheddeth man's blood, by man shall his blood be shed: for in the image of God made he man." Only blood was payment for blood because man was made in God's image.

This law precedes the Law of Moses and was not cancelled out in the Old or New Testament. God forbids the willful killing of one man by another. This includes abortion, but does not include the killing in war, self-defense, or an accidental killing.

In ancient times, six cities of refuge were established for those who killed in self-defense or accidently (Numbers 35:6-34). These cities were established as a place they could go in order to escape the blood avenger, who was duty-bound to avenge the shedding of innocent blood. The blood avenger could not kill them if they remained in one of these cities.

Clearly, God established capital punishment. This was also understood by the Israelites under the Levitical Law. Numbers 35:29-34 tells us why it was necessary to avenge innocent blood: "So you shall not pollute the land wherein you are: for blood it defileth the land; and the land cannot be cleansed of the blood that is shed therein, but by the blood of him that shed it. Defile not therefore the land which ye shall inhabit."

So, we learn in Numbers what happens when we do not put murderers to death. *We pollute and defile our land.* And Deuteronomy 19:13 warns us that "Thine eye shall not pity him (the murderer) but thou shall put away the guilt of innocent blood from Israel that it may go well with thee."

If the guilt of innocent blood is not put away, if the murderer is not made to pay with his blood, it will not go well with that nation!

Many well-meaning Christians are opposed to capital punishment. But they are considering only how they view the matter and how they feel rather than what God says. Proverbs 3:5-6 warns, "lean not unto thine own understanding, in all thy ways acknowledge Him (God) and He shall direct thy paths." In the end, it doesn't matter what we think is right, it only matters what God says is right. We need to align our thinking with God's Word because God is never going to align His with ours.

## So, we know that

God Himself instituted the death penalty. That only blood can pay for the shedding of innocent blood. That we are not to pity the murderer. And if a murderer does not pay with his blood that land becomes defiled and polluted, and it will not go well for that nation.

Murder is still forbidden in the New Testament (Matthew 19:18, Romans 13:9, 1Peter 4:15, 1 John 3:15). But what happens if the murderer accepts Jesus? Well, he'll still have to face the consequences set forth in that nation's legal system. But spiritually speaking, if that murderer confesses his sin and puts it under the blood of Jesus, Jesus' blood satisfies the requirements of the blood avenger and that sin will not be held against that nation.

## After Noah, the next blood episode is in Genesis 15:7-18

After God tells Abraham that he will inherit the promised land, He instructs him to offer a sacrifice, which Abraham does by cutting up several animals and laying the pieces side by side with a path in between. When a blood covenant was cut in ancient times, both parties would walk together between the pieces. What they were saying was: "may this be done to me if I break this covenant".

Note that only after the animal sacrifice is made does that promise become a covenant. God's pledge in Genesis 15:7 "to give" Abraham the promised land becomes "have I given" in Genesis 15:18. The transaction is complete! It moves from a future promise to a present one.

But it's also interesting to note that only God, coming as a "smoking furnace and a burning lamp" passed between the pieces. Abraham never did, indicating that the covenant did not hinge on Abraham's future actions, but only on God's faithfulness. This, along with numerous other scriptures such as the eleventh chapter of Romans, completely negates the erroneous teaching of replacement theology which says we have taken Israel's place. It's a theology deeply rooted in anti-Semitism and began by church leaders such as Eusebius of Caesarea

(265-339 A.D.) and Saint Augustine (354-430 A.D.) and embraced by the Catholic Church. But unfortunately, it now seems to be gaining increasingly wider acceptance among Protestant churches, as well.

Yes, we have been grafted in and can enjoy the same blessings God promised Abraham, but God is **not** finished with the Jews or the nation of Israel, and the Church has **not** taken their place. During the tribulation, which is also called the Day of Jacob's Trouble, God will cleanse them and prepare them for their Messiah, Jesus, as well as to prepare them to become the **head** of nations. Because Jesus is coming back to Jerusalem, not Washington D.C. or Paris, or Rome, or any place else.

## Our next blood encounter: Genesis 22:1-19

where God asks Abraham to sacrifice his son, Isaac. This is a beautiful foreshadowing of God's love and plan. First, God tells Abraham to take Isaac to a mountain He would show him, in order to sacrifice his son. It turned out to be Mt. Moriah, which is significant. 2 Chronicles 3:1 says, "Then Solomon began to build the house of the Lord at Jerusalem in Mt. Moriah." Mt. Moriah was the future site of the Temple, the Holy of Holies, and all the blood sacrifices that would be made under the Levitical Law, as well as the area where Jesus would be sacrificed.

Next, God calls Isaac, "thine *only* son, Isaac, whom thou *lovest*." God calls him this knowing Ishmael was Abraham's first born. But Ishmael was not the son of promise, while Isaac was a type of Jesus, a foreshadowing of the *only* begotten Son Whom God *loved*.

Genesis 22:6 says, "And Abraham took the wood of the burnt offering and laid it upon Isaac his son". Picture Isaac carrying the bundle of wood for the sacrifice on his shoulder just as Jesus, in obedience to God the Father, carried the wooden cross or beam upon which he would be sacrificed. Scholars believe Isaac was a young man and not a child when this occurred, yet he went along obediently. Isaac, like Jesus, was prepared to be obedient unto death.

We can only imagine Abraham's grief at the thought of having to kill his beloved son; a foreshadowing of God the Father's grief as He allowed His perfect, holy, spotless Son to become the blood sacrifice of the new covenant!

It is interesting to note the prophetic nature of Abraham's response when Isaac asked, "where is the lamb for a burnt offering?" In Genesis 22:8 we read his answer, "And Abraham said, My son, God will provide himself a lamb for a burnt offering." But Abraham wasn't just talking about the ram he found caught in a thicket and killed in place of Isaac. Since it was a ram, not a lamb, it only partially fulfilled the prophecy. What Abraham was prophetically referring to was the fact that God was going to provide **Himself**, in the form of Jesus, as the Lamb without spot or blemish, to be slain for the sins of the world!

## Next, the Passover (Exodus 12:1-13)

Moses has been sent by God to deliver his people who had been in Egypt for four hundred years. But Pharaoh proves difficult.

He vacillates about letting them go. Nine plagues have fallen on Egypt. Now, the tenth and final plague, and the worst, will be the slaying of all first-born males, both man and animal.

To protect his people from the angel of death, God instructs Moses to have each household take a male lamb, without spot or blemish, in other words, perfect, and put the blood of this lamb on the door posts and door frame of each house. In Exodus 12:12 God tells Moses, "I will pass through the land of Egypt this night and will smite all the firstborn in the land of Egypt, both man and beast."

Note that God didn't say all firstborn Egyptians, but all the firstborn in the land both man and beast. What protected the Israelites? Exodus 12:13 tells us: "And the blood shall be to you for a token upon the houses where ye are: and when I see the blood, I will pass over you, and the plague shall not be upon you to destroy you, when I smite the land of Egypt."

It wasn't the fact that they were Israelites that saved them but that the blood of an innocent lamb was applied to their door posts and door frames, causing the angel of death to "pass over" them. Hence the name of the Jewish feast.

This is, once again, a foreshadowing that only blood could save. And a foreshadowing of Jesus, the perfect Lamb of God, the Lamb without spot or blemish. It's a foreshadowing of His blood applied to the door posts of our hearts when we accept Him, causing us to pass from spiritual death into eternal life.

## The next blood episode: the giving of the commandments

God will end up giving these commandments three different times. Three is the number of the Trinity and illustrates the God-Head.

The first time is in Exodus 19-24. Here, God speaks from the mountain top. Only Moses, and Aaron, the future High Priest, can approach Him. The rest of the people will die if they touch the mountain. This speaks of God the Father, how, since the fall of Adam,

His holiness made Him distance Himself from mankind. It's also the foreshadowing that only a High Priest may enter His presence in the Holy of Holy. Even so, His heart yearned to reconcile man back to Himself and become our Father, Abba, Daddy.

The second time is in Exodus 31. Here, the commandments are made tangible, carved on tablets of stone, something that can be handled, touched. This speaks of Jesus who came as a tangible man, to be handled and touched. He was the very WORD made flesh coming to fulfil the law. But before Moses even gets off the mountain, the law is broken, showing man is incapable of keeping God's laws and that the remedy is Jesus who, like the tables of stone, will also be broken at the cross.

And the third time is in Exodus 34 where Moses gets another set of tablets, which remain intact. When he comes down the mountain this time, his face shines from being in the presence of God. This is a foreshadowing of the Holy Spirit and the future covenant of grace, and how only through the Holy Spirit are we capable of keeping the commandments.

But after God gives Israel the commandments the first time, Moses, in Exodus 24:1-8 builds an altar. In order to seal this covenant with God and the people, Moses has the young men offer animal sacrifices. He takes the blood and sprinkles half of it on the altar. Then Moses does something amazing. After reading the covenant, he sprinkles the other half of the blood on the **people**, and says, "Behold the blood of the covenant, which the Lord hath made with you concerning all these words."

This is extraordinary when you remember that blood is reserved only for God and this is the first time that people have any part in it. Now, half of the blood is sprinkled on them directly.

## Next

is the consecration of Aaron and his sons into the priesthood (Exodus 29:1-35). Aaron is from the tribe of Levi and all Temple workers will come from that line. But all future priests are to come directly from Aaron's line. And part of the consecration into the priesthood involved applying the blood of the sacrificed animal directly to the tip of the priest's right ear, signifying his ability to hear God's voice; upon the right thumb, signifying his obedience in serving God; and upon the big toe of the right foot, signifying he would walk in God's ways. The rest of the blood, along with the anointing oil, was sprinkled over their garments and on the altar.

It is interesting to note that in the Old Testament, leprosy was symbolic of sin. According to Leviticus 13, a leper was isolated and couldn't live with the rest of the population. And whenever he came upon a non-leprous person he had to cry "unclean, unclean". In essence, the leper was dead.

It's a picture of the sinner who is unclean in the sight of God and dead in his sins. And like leprosy, sin separates us from God and others. Also, like leprosy, secret sin can be hidden from others for years. Then it manifests, beginning like a small patch of raised skin before spreading and affecting the flesh, and finally, the bones. It was progressive, like sin, which can eat away at a life, devouring it. And just as leprosy was disfiguring, so sin disfigures a life, keeping a person from being all God wants him to be.

The illustration of leprosy shows how terrible sin is. How it affects the lives of not only those who sin but their families. When a person had leprosy, it changed the dynamics of that entire family. Just like sin can change the dynamics of an entire family. And like leprosy, sin can be contagious when we hang out with the wrong crowd, fill our mind with wrong books, TV programs, movies, music, video games, because they can all produce an inclination toward sin.

When we really see how terrible leprosy was, how it marred and disfigured a life, how it isolated and separated a person, then we begin to understand how God views sin.

But here's the interesting part. In the ritual cleansing of a leper, the blood of an animal was applied in **exactly** the same manner as blood was applied during the consecration of a priest: to the right ear, right thumb and right big toe. But these same places were also anointed with oil, something not done to the Levitical priests. Their ear, thumb and big toe were not anointed with oil.

So, here we see, in the cleansing of a leper, a foreshadowing of those cleansed of sin by the blood of Jesus, and in the process, they become priests! 1 Peter 2:5 says we are a "holy priesthood". And 1 Peter 2:9 says, "But ye are a chosen generation, a royal priesthood, an holy nation, a peculiar people that ye should shew forth the **praises** of him who hath called you out of darkness into his marvelous light."

We no longer need a high priest. We are God's priests, and the sacrifices we offer Him are our praises.

In the New Testament, oil is representative of the Holy Spirit. So, regarding the oil applied to the leper, it's the promise of the Holy Spirit's empowerment. By listening (the ear) to, and being guided by the Holy Spirit, we will be empowered to do (the thumb) the work He wants us to do and go (the toe) wherever He wants us to go! Amazing!

## The Day of Atonement: Exodus 30:10

God commands that, "Aaron shall make an atonement upon the horns of it (the altar) once in a year with the blood of the sin offering of atonements; once in the year shall he make atonement upon it throughout your generations: it is most holy unto the Lord."

So, once a year, according to Leviticus 16, to atone for the sins of the nation of Israel, the High Priest went into the Holy of Holies where the ark of the covenant stood, and poured lamb's blood over the mercy seat. The ark of the covenant was a wooden box covered in gold with a gold lid flanked by two golden angels, one on each end. And the space on the gold lid between the two angels was the mercy seat.

Only a High Priest could enter the Holy of Holies. And only after he had ritually purified himself. You can imagine he did this with much fear and trembling because if he or his sacrifice were not acceptable, he would die on the spot. Since only a High Priest could enter the Holy of Holies this presented a problem. How were they to get the dead body out should this happen? The solution: small bells were sewn around the skirt of the High Priest's garment and a rope tied around his ankle. As long as those outside could hear the bells jingling while the High Priest moved around performing his duty, they knew he was alive. But if the bells stopped for any length of time they would yank on the rope, and if the priest had died, they would pull him out.

Leviticus details numerous other types of animal sacrifices for individual sins, showing the cleansing of sin to be a very bloody and violent act. And it again shows how serious sin is to God. It was also a prelude to the brutal, violent, bloody act of crucifixion where sin would be, once and for all, dealt with, not as a sin covering, like putting a clean shirt over a dirty garment and covering it up, as in the Old Testament, but a total forgiveness and cleansing of sin under the new covenant.

Following the Blood Trail

# Chapter 3

# Following the Blood Trail in the New Testament

In Matthew 26:17-30 Jesus is celebrating the Passover with His disciples, and it says, "And as they were eating, Jesus took bread, and blessed it, and brake it, and gave it to the disciples and said, Take, eat, this is my body. And he took the cup and gave thanks, and gave it to them saying, Drink ye all of it, For this is my blood of the new testament, which is shed for many for the remission of sins."

In these passages, Jesus is telling them to eat his body and *drink* his blood. We must understand how radical a statement this was and how horrifying this was to a Jew. Remember, drinking blood was forbidden in the Hebrew religion.

In John 6:53-58 we see Jesus telling his disciples that "Except ye eat the flesh of the Son of man and drink his blood, ye have no life in you. Whoso eateth my flesh and drinketh my blood, hath eternal life; and I will raise him up at the last day."

It goes on to say in John 6:66, "From that time many of his disciples went back, and walked no more with him." Why? Because it was simply too radical, and in their mind, blasphemy! That's because they didn't understand what Jesus really meant.

## And what Jesus said was radical

We know God's requirement was that innocent blood had to be shed for the remission of sins, a requirement He established back in the Garden of Eden, and which was clearly understood in both the Old and New Testament.

In fact, Hebrews 9:22, in the New Testament, says, "And almost all things are by the law purged with blood; and without shedding of blood is no remission." So, again we are told that without the shedding of blood there is no remission of sins!

But what no one could imagine is that God Himself would provide that innocent blood, that it would be **His** blood. If we really think about it, we can understand why it had to be His. What mere man would be worthy enough to do this? What man is "without spot or blemish"? For all men are tainted by sin.

And Jesus never meant that we were to actually drink His blood. All through Scripture blood has represented life. What Jesus was saying was that if we accepted the shedding of His blood as **our** sin sacrifice, we could pass from spiritual death into spiritual life.

In addition, God wasn't just going to sprinkle the blood on us or anoint parts of our body. He was offering to share His very life with us through His indwelling Holy Spirit.

The story of Ruth, in the Old Testament, is the story of the kinsman redeemer. It sets up the standard that only a relative could redeem that which was lost. That's why Jesus had to come in the flesh, to become our kinsman, our relative.

And by telling them to eat the bread, His flesh, Jesus was saying that He was the Bread of Life. It was no accident that He was born in Bethlehem, which, in Hebrew, means House of Bread. He **is** the bread that nourishes and sustains us. He **is** the manna sent from heaven. The manna given to the Israelites during their forty years in the wilderness was but a foreshadowing of Jesus. But how do we eat the Bread of Life? The apostle John called Jesus the WORD made flesh. So, we are to ingest His Word. It's His Word that sustains, guides, and heals us. It's His Word that changes us.

Psalm 34:8 says, "Oh taste and see that the Lord is good". Again, we taste God by studying His word. By making it part of us, part of our lives. Through His word, we understand how truly good God is.

Romans 8:1-5, written after Jesus' death and resurrection, says, "There is therefore now no condemnation to them which are in Christ Jesus". Why? Because, Jesus' blood was a once and for all perfect sacrifice. It covered **all** our sins and became the basis for the new contract between God and man.

## Jesus becomes the Passover lamb

Every day, the Temple priests offered two lambs: one in the morning when the trumpets were blown to announce the first sacrifice of the day and the doors of the Temple were opened; and one in the afternoon, indicating the last sacrifice of the day. In between, for six hours, the priests would oversee the individual sacrifices made by the people for their sins.

At the exact time the priests were offering the first lamb of the day, which was the third hour or 9 a.m., Jesus was crucified. And He hung on the cross six hours, during the very six hours when people brought their personal sacrifices to the Temple. During this time, He became sin for us, taking on all our shame, guilt, and emotional anguish. Then, at the exact time when the priests offered the second and last lamb of the day, which was the ninth hour or 3 p.m., Jesus died.

As mentioned before, it was no accident that Jesus, the Bread of Life, was born in Bethlehem, the House of Bread. Neither was it a coincidence that during those days, in the area around Bethlehem, there was a place called the tower of Edar which literally means the tower of the flock. Why is this important? Because it was here that the flock of lambs for the Temple sacrifices were born, raised and tended. Scholars believe that it was to these very shepherds that the angel appeared, announcing Jesus' birth. It was these very shepherds who then went to see the newly born Lamb of God in the manger!

Jesus also shed His blood seven times. In the Bible, seven is the number of perfection and completion, such as seven days of creation, seven golden lampstands, seven churches, the seven seals, seven trumpets, etcetera.

Sylvia Bambola

The first time Jesus shed His blood is during the agony in the garden where he sweat "great drops of blood" (Luke 22:44). Second: when they tore off His beard and struck Him in the face (Isaiah 50:6; Luke 22:63-65). Third: the whipping post when he received thirty-nine lashes that split open his back. Fourth: when Jesus was crowned with thorns and the soldiers beat Him over the head with a reed, driving the thorns deeper (Matthew 27:29-30). Fifth: when they nailed His hands to the cross; hands that had healed so many. Sixth: when they nailed His feet to the cross; feet that walked the dust of the earth as He tried to show us how to live. And seventh: when the soldier pierced His side, and blood and water came out.

Jesus gave it all.

There was nothing left for Him to give. And just before He died, He said, "IT IS FINISHED". That word in Greek is *teleo* and means completed, **paid in full**. Jesus paid the penalty for all our sins in full. He completely satisfied God's requirements, God's holiness and God's justice. And it wasn't a cover-up of sin like in the Old Testament, but a complete cleansing and forgiveness.

In ancient times, rabbis believed there would be two Messiahs: Messiah ben Joseph, the suffering servant, and Messiah ben David, the king. They were nearly right. But instead of two Messiahs, there would only be One; One who would come twice. During Jesus' first coming He fulfilled the role of Messiah Ben Joseph, the suffering servant. He suffered rejection by His brothers and laid down His life as a ransom for ours.

It gives Jesus the right to say, "I am **the** way, **the** truth and **the** life, no man comes to the Father but through me" (John 14:6). There are not many ways to God. There is only one. And that way is Jesus.

And this blood requirement and Jesus' blood payment are very different from the concept of earning our salvation. The Bible clearly states salvation cannot be earned. Ephesians 2:8-9 says, "For by grace are ye saved through faith; and that not of yourselves: it is a gift of God not of works, lest any man should boast."

We do good works because we love God, not because we are trying to work our way to heaven or get God to love us. He already does! He already loves us completely and totally!

## The empty tomb

In John 20:1-12 Mary Magdalene goes to the tomb and sees that it's empty. The tomb was carved out of rock with a rock slab where the dead body was laid. Mary also sees two angels in white, one sitting at the head of the burial slab and the other at the foot. Imagine that in between the two was Jesus' blood that had seeped through the linen cloth that wrapped Him. What she was seeing was symbolic of the ark of the covenant with the two angels on each end and the bloody mercy seat in the middle.

Then, she sees Jesus. He tells her in John 20:17, **"Touch me not**; for I am not yet ascended to my Father: but go to my brethren and say unto them, I ascend unto my Father and your Father; and to my God and your God." But a few verses later (John 20:26-29) we see Jesus telling Thomas to **touch Him**. What happened in between?

Hebrews 5:6, 10 tells us that Jesus is a High Priest after the Order of Melchisedec. So, in between, Jesus had to ascend to His Father and perform his High Priestly function and pour His blood on the Mercy Seat in the heavenly temple. The Jewish temple, ark of the covenant, altar of incense, menorah, etcetera, were all replicas of what exists in heaven.

Under Levitical Law, a High Priest couldn't touch or be touched by anything unclean prior to offering sacrifices to God. One can only assume it applies to the Order of Melchisedec, too. That's why Mary couldn't touch Jesus. And according to Hebrews 7:24-28, Jesus continues as our High Priest even today.

## And finally, the great deed transfer

In the Book of Revelation (chapters 5-6) John is caught up to heaven and sees God holding a scroll. The scroll has seven seals. Then an angel shouts, "Who is worthy to open the book and to loose the seals thereof?"

When no one is found, John begins to weep. But then Revelation 5:6-7 says, "and in the midst of the elders, stood a Lamb as it had been slain, having seven horns and seven eyes, which are the seven Spirits of God sent forth into all the earth. And he came and took the book out of the right hand of him that sat upon the throne." Then thunderous praise breaks out.

What's happening? Jesus is preparing to return as Messiah bed David, the King of Kings and Lord of Lords! He is taking back the title deed of the earth! It's the title deed Satan, as the watchman, was once entrusted with before his rebellion; the title deed Adam and Eve once had before they sinned and transferred their authority back to Satan, making him the "god of this world". The deed now belongs to Jesus because he became our kinsman redeemer and paid for it with His blood. And He's now ready to claim His property.

As Jesus opens each of the seven seals, a new judgment is unleashed, each designed to cleanse the earth and prepare it for His earthly 1000-year reign. The opening of the seals begins the seven-year tribulation. It will be a horrendous time on earth. Satan's true nature will finally be fully exposed. There will be no doubt left in the minds of the remaining holy angels of Satan's true character. And everything that can be shaken will be shaken. In the end, only Jesus and righteousness will be left standing.

What a wonder God is! He has given us so much. And in doing so, has forever put to rest all questions of His character, His love, kindness, His fairness, His patience and long suffering. And when this age is over, after the seven-year tribulation and 1000-year reign of Jesus, when time has run out and there is only eternity, no angel, no demon, no man, no woman will be able to cast doubts about Him again. For all He will have to do is point back to the corridor of time as His witness.

# Chapter 4

# But what does that mean for us now?

Well, nothing for those who reject Jesus. They will continue down the same path they are already on, heading for hell. Yes, hell is real. And they'll continue to be vulnerable to the arbitrary and every changing dictates of the world. And they will be susceptible to the wiles of the devil. That's why it's so important that Christians pray and witness, not only in words but by actions and examples.

But those who do acknowledge they are sinners in need of a savior because they can't save themselves, and who accept what

Jesus did for them and then invite Him to take control of their lives, they become **new** creatures, old things are passed away and all things become new (2 Corinthians 5:17)! They can enter the very Holy of Holies themselves! They can enter God's presence and commune with Him.

In fact, immediately after Jesus died, Matthew 27:51 tells us that the veil of the temple was torn in two from the top to the bottom. The veil he is talking about is the veil that separated the Holy of Holies from the Holy Place. This veil was so thick and strong, it is said it would have taken a team of oxen to rip it in two. The fact that it was torn in half from top to bottom indicates that God Himself tore it, thus removing the barrier into His presence. The Bible tells us that we can now "come boldly before His throne." We become His priests and have open access to Him.

But what Jesus did means so much more. We now have powerful weapons of warfare to fight all the spiritual battles we will encounter in life. Because spiritual warfare is a study in itself, only a brief summary is presented here:

**The blood of Jesus** which frightens demonic powers because this is what defeated them.

**The Name of Jesus**: At the name of Jesus every knee will bow, including Satan's.

**The Word of God**: When Jesus was tempted in the wilderness for forty days and nights, He used scripture to combat Satan's attacks.

**Praise**, which is very powerful because the Bible says that God inhabits the praises of His people.

**And Prayer**

I'd like to share one example of how I used the blood of Jesus, the name of Jesus and the Word of God in the past.

Growing up, I had strep throat a few times but then in my early thirties, I began getting them on a regular basis. Antibiotics helped for a while, but then I'd get sick all over again. It was a cycle that was wearing me down. After enjoying a few months of good health, I woke up feeling the familiar symptoms. I was achy, feverish, tired. My throat was sore and burning. When I checked it out in the mirror and saw the familiar white dots lining the back of my throat, I felt deflated. My two young children needed attention. Plus, there were the demands of running a household. I could not face another day on the couch.

I had been learning about the power of Jesus' blood and His Word, and in desperation, I laid hands on my throat, and in Jesus' name and by faith, covered it with His blood, then claimed God's Word over me saying, "By Jesus' stripes I **am** healed." I wish I could say I felt better, but I didn't. I felt every bit as sick as before. Still, I continued praying this throughout the day. And by 5 p.m., I felt completely well! And when I checked my throat, every white speck was gone! And from that day to this, I have never had another strep throat. Praise God!

That day, I learned the importance of finding the scriptures pertaining to a given situation and then, in faith, speaking them over myself. And there are plenty of scriptures covering every need.

If fear arises, I declare, "I can do all things through Christ who strengthens me, and I have not been given a spirit of fear but of power and love and a sound mind"

When I'm feeling unsure about God's love, I declare, "God loves me with an everlasting love, He will never leave me or forsake me."

When I don't feel strong enough to walk in God's ways, I declare, "It's not by might nor by power but by my Spirit says the Lord," reminding me that it is the Holy Spirit Who empowers and enables me to do God's will, not me.

There is an answer for everything in God's Word. And it's not a "name-it-and-claim-it" scheme. It's about standing on God's promises and believing His Word, and believing His Word is still for us today, then waiting for God to fulfil it in His own prefect timing. When I was battling strep throat, I had to wait several hours to receive my healing. I've heard testimonies of how other people stood on God's Word for months and sometimes years before it came to pass. Our job is to STAND on God's word. God's job is to DO it.

And speaking of words, they matter. It matters what we say about ourselves as well as what we say about others. Proverbs 18:21 says, "life and death are in the power of the tongue," meaning words have both creative and destructive power. Also, Matthew 12:36 tells us that we will have to give an accounting for every idle we speak. Ouch! We need to watch our words and speak life. Always life. And when we do, we are partnering with God and allowing Him to work His will in our lives.

Now for praise.

I find praise so powerful because God inhabits the praises of His people. Praise is a way of ushering in His presence. Praise is what got me through the tough times after my husband died. Even when I was sad and didn't feel like it, I'd praise God. And before I knew it, I'd feel His presence. And then, slowly joy would begin to bubble up inside. God never failed. If I was willing to praise Him in the midst of my pain, He would always show up. I'd also play praise music throughout the day because it created a wonderful atmosphere. If God inhabits the praises of His people, why wouldn't it?

I believe praise is the remedy when we feel down or stressed or troubled. It's one of the best weapons we have against these things. Satan likes nothing better than to get us to feel sorry for ourselves, to get us to have a big pity party. That's because when we do, we focus on ourselves. We become self-absorbed instead of God-absorbed. And that is when Satan can defeat us.

And finally, there's prayer. There are many types of prayer which, again, is for another study, but for me, praying in tongues is one of the most powerful in spiritual warfare.

There are two types of tongues.

The first is the kind spoken at Pentecost when the disciples spoke authentic languages; languages they had never spoken before; languages understood by the various visitors in Jerusalem at the time.

Then, there is the type of tongues which usually makes no sense to the speaker or hearer (unless there is an interpretation of tongues) but is what the Bible describes as the groanings and utterings of the Holy

Spirit when He helps us to pray because we don't know how to.

I have never experienced the first type but know of people who have when on a mission field. While there, they began speaking in a foreign language which they didn't understand and had never learned, but which turned out to be the language of that nation and was a blessing to many hearers.

But the second type of tongues I am familiar with, and find it a valuable weapon in my spiritual warfare arsenal because sometimes God puts a person on my heart and has me pray for him/her. Most of the time, I have no clue what's going on in that person's life or why he/she needs prayer. But God knows. And through His Holy Spirit, I begin to moan and speak words that sound unintelligible to me. A few times, God has given me the interpretation and I know exactly what I'm saying, but most of the time I don't. Even so, when I pray this way, I feel a spirit of warfare rise in me and know that I am doing battle in the heavenlies. It's very powerful.

But no one has to pray in tongues if they don't want to. The thing is, we get to.

Satan also has false tongues. He tries to mimic everything God does. I've only encountered this once when I was a guest speaker at a women's luncheon. A woman, who had, over the past several months, firmly attached herself to the pastor's wife, insisted that she lay hands on me and pray. I sensed in my spirit that something was wrong and midway in prayer had to stop her. There was a definite evil presence about her. I learned months later that the church had split due to this woman.

I share this as a warning. At the time the above happened, I still believed everyone in church was there because they loved God or at least wanted to know Him more. But God showed me that's not true. We need to be aware of who is laying hands on us or who we allow to pray over us. In short, we must be sensitive to the Holy Spirit. There could be a witch or warlock, posing as a Christian, but sent by their local coven to destroy that church. It's more common than you might think. But that's another subject.

Also, we need to understand that all churches have their traditions. Most are fine. But some teach things that aren't scriptural, like saying tongues aren't real or that miracles ended when the apostles died. But that's not what the Bible says. I began praying in tongues before anyone taught me about it or told me it wasn't for today. And people are being raised from the dead in Africa because the Christians there have child-like faith! And what about those in strict Muslim countries who are coming to Jesus because of dreams and visions? So, contrary to some church's traditions, God is still working according to His Word.

Unfortunately, many western Christians feel they are too intelligent or sophisticated to believe in such things. And this hinders God's ability to perform miracles. Remember how Jesus was unable to do many miracles in His hometown because of unbelief? It still applies.

When the traditions of a church contradict God's Word we must **always** come down on the side of God's Word. Jesus was kind to sinners. But to the religious crowd, he was harsh. He said they made void the Word of

God by their traditions. He called them "whitewashed sepulchers full of dead men's bones", meaning they looked great on the outside but inside they were spiritually dead. He also called them hypocrites.

We need to believe God's Word and appropriate everything Jesus did for us. But because Jesus gave everything for us, we should give everything for Him. The apostle John, in John 3:30, said, "He (meaning Jesus) must increase, but I must decrease." That should be our prayer, too. We should desire that Jesus become more and more evident in our lives while our own selfish nature becomes less and less.

And we should never let anyone define us. Nor are we to define ourselves. Only Jesus, who bought and paid for us with His blood, has a right to do that. We need to see ourselves as God sees us. The Bible says, in Proverbs 23:7, that as a man thinks in his heart so is he. What does that mean? It means that if we focus on what others say about us or how we feel about our own shortcomings and be constantly saying, "I'm not good at this or I can't do that, or I don't like this about myself, or this is wrong with me, etcetera, it becomes a self-fulfilling prophecy. We are, actually cursing ourselves. Remember, life and death are in the power of the tongue. Again, we need to see ourselves as God sees us, and to say about ourselves what God says about us.

And what does He say about us?

God said He will never leave us or forsake us. He said His Holy Spirit will comfort, teach, guide and empower us. And that the totality of salvation is ours, which means we are not only saved from hell, but have divine protection, provision, deliverance, and health.

He says we are a child of God; a new creation in Christ. We are His workmanship. He's the one who is going to make us a masterpiece. Philippians 1:6 says, "Being confident of this very thing, that he which hath begun a good work in you will perform it until the day of Jesus Christ." God is the one doing the good work in us. And He's not going to give up on us, either!

Also, God says we are the temple of the Holy Spirit. We are God's friend. We are the head and not the tail. We are blessed coming in and going out. We are wonderfully made. We have not been given a spirit of fear but of power and love and a sound mind. God says He loves us with an everlasting love. That we are royalty; we are kings and priests. That we are joint heirs with Christ, meaning all that He has is ours. And we are part of the Bride of Christ, and we will be with Him forever.

Every one of these are true. Yet, believe it or not, there are even more. We need to walk in our God-given authority and our God-given identity, so we can fulfil our God-given assignment on earth. But we have free will and can choose to believe what God says about us or we can believe what the world or others or what we say about ourselves.

But if we choose wrong, we are going to miss out on so much of what God has for us.

www.ingramcontent.com/pod-product-compliance
Lightning Source LLC
Chambersburg PA
CBHW060714030426
42337CB00017B/2865